DRAW WITH PENNY

Claire Llewellyn
Lisa Austin

Contents

Penny!

I am Penny the Pencil.

I can draw:

- a bird
- a car
- a funny face

You can draw them too.
Let me show you.

Bird

Look at the bird.

Can you see shapes in the bird?
We can draw them.

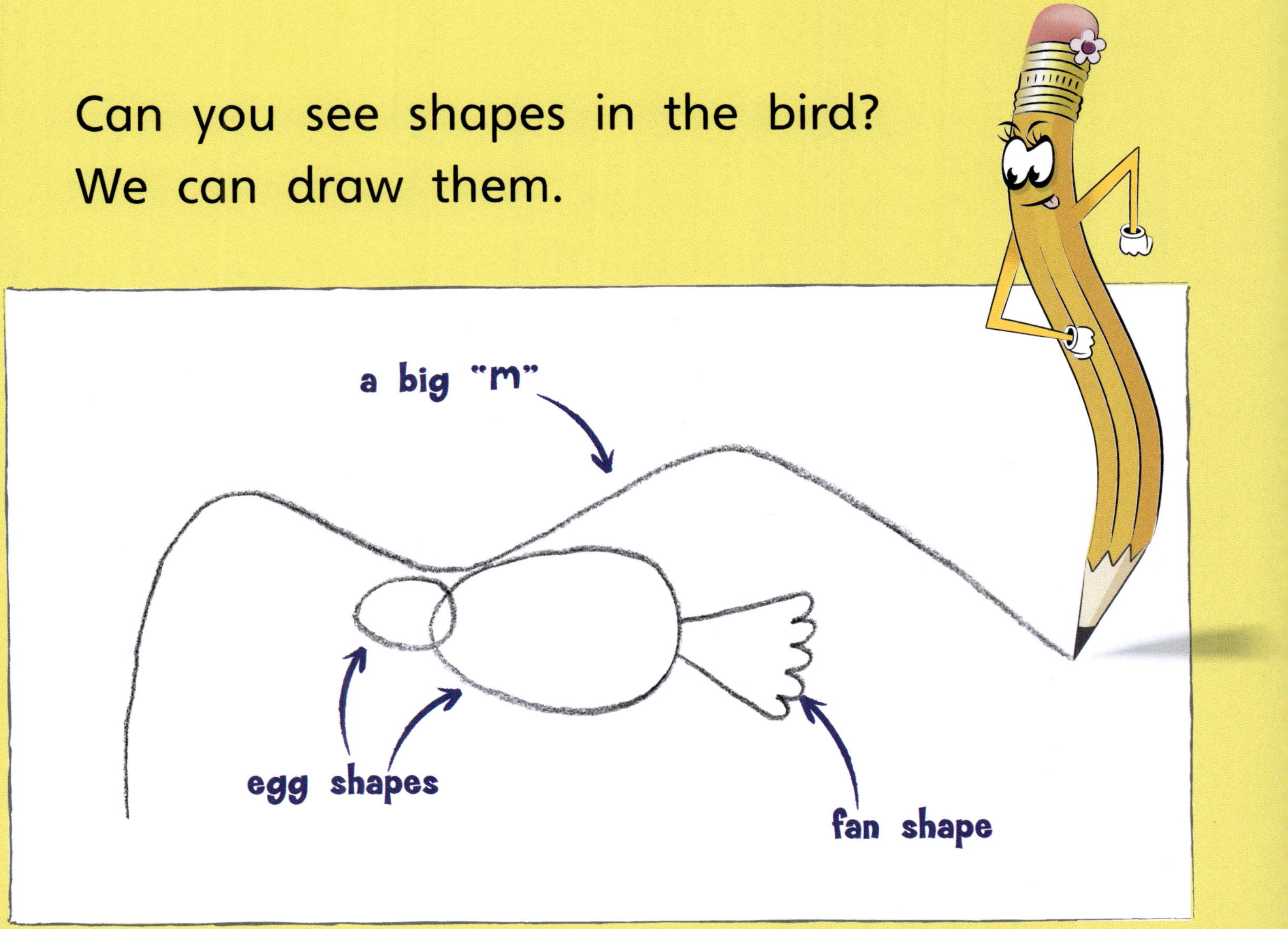

Draw a BIRD

1 Draw an egg shape.

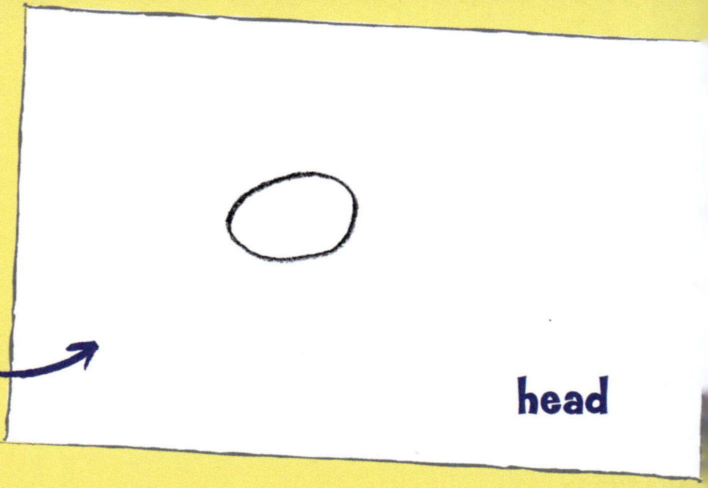

2 Now draw a big egg shape.

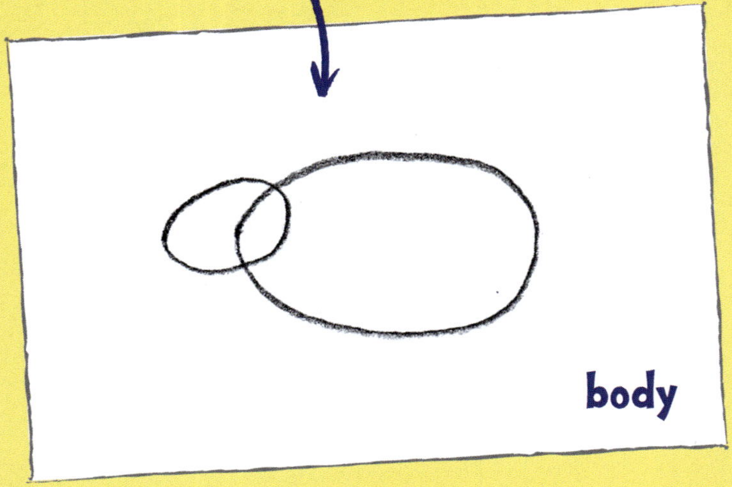

3 Draw a fan shape.

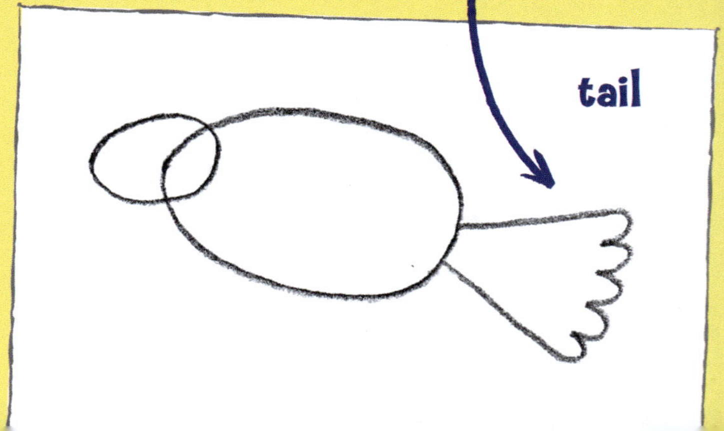

4 Draw a big “M”.

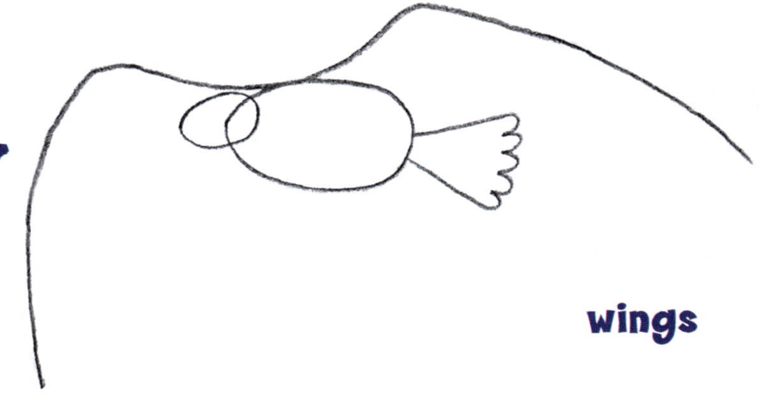

5 Now add the beak and the feet.

It is a bird!

Car

Look at the car.

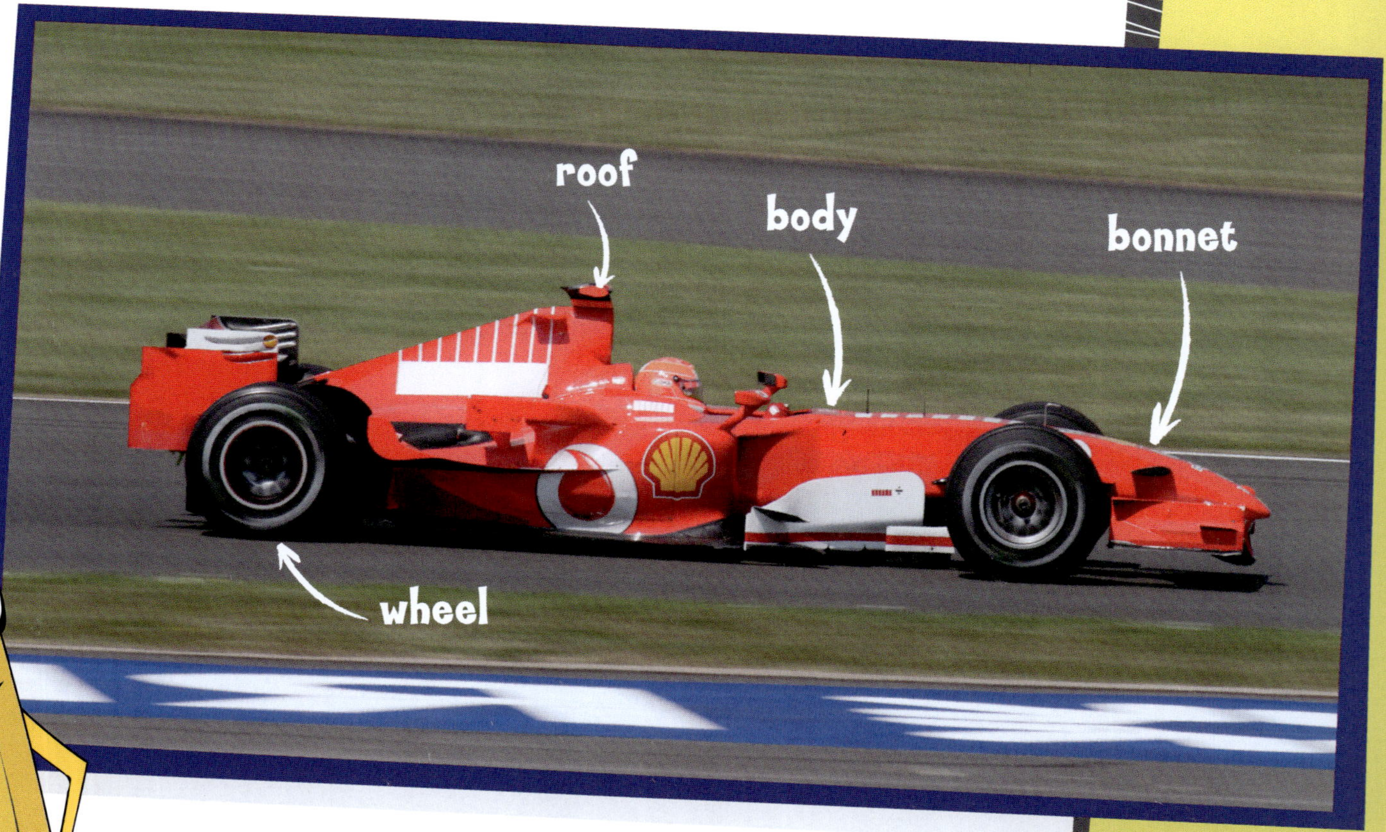

Can you see shapes in the car?
We can draw them.

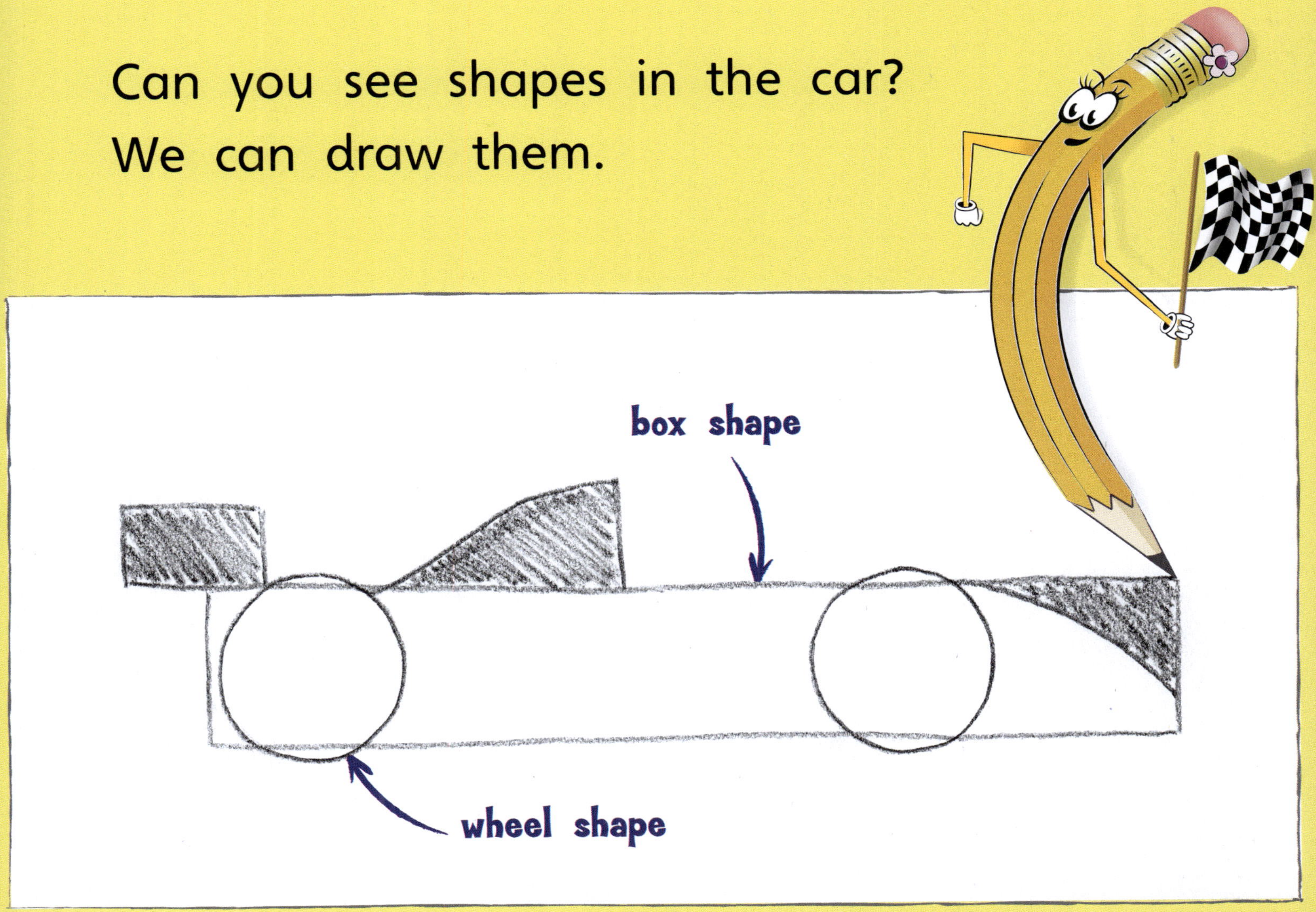

Draw a CAR

1 Draw a box.

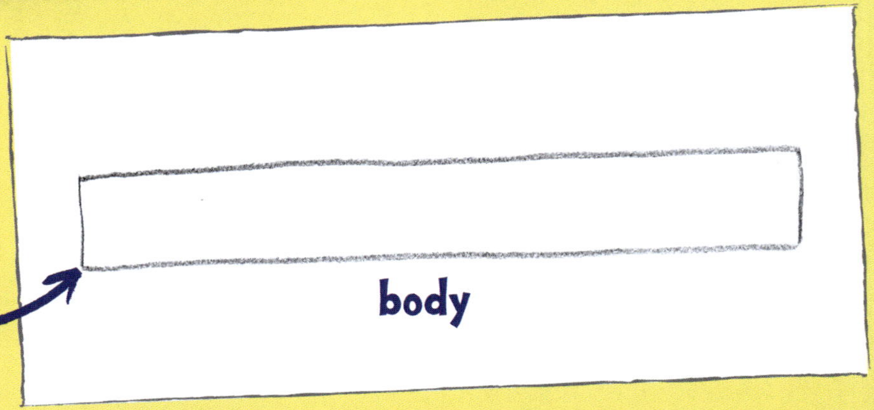

2 Draw the wheels.

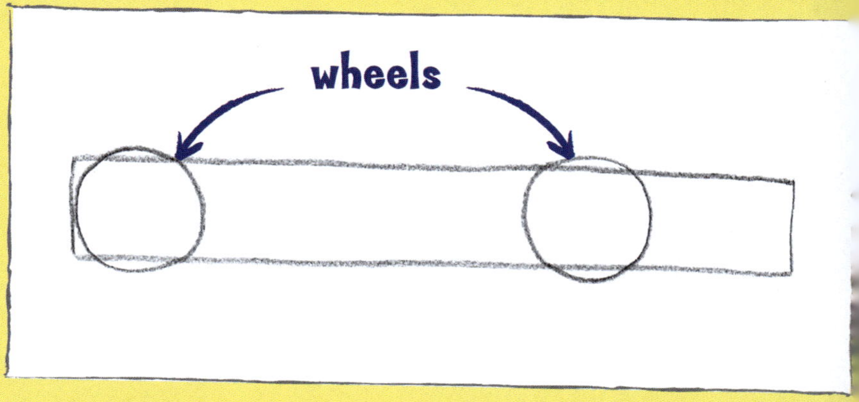

3 Add the bonnet.

4 Add the roof.

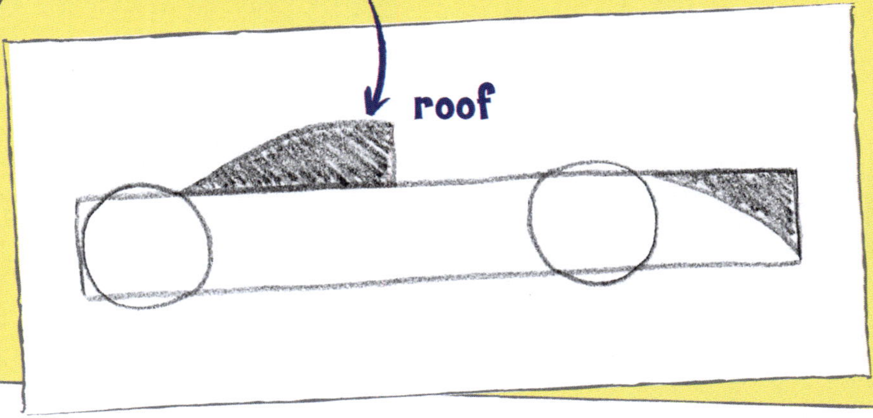

It is a car!

Funny Face

Look at the funny face.

Can you see the shapes in it?
We can draw them.

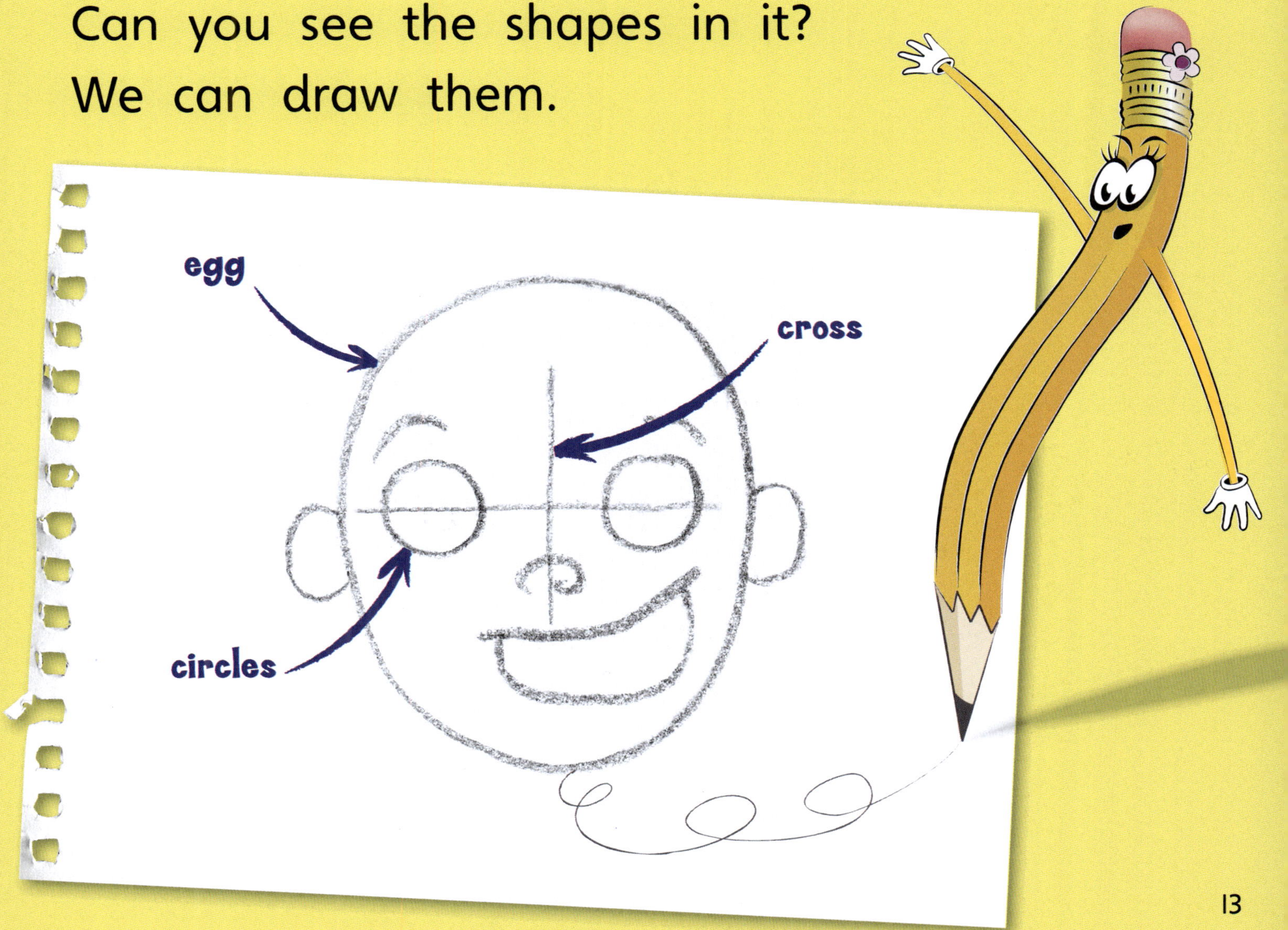

Draw a FUNNY FACE

1 Draw an egg shape.

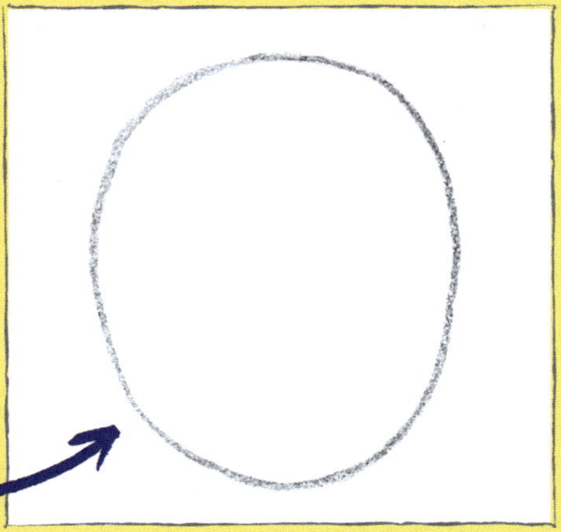

2 Draw a cross for the eyes and nose.

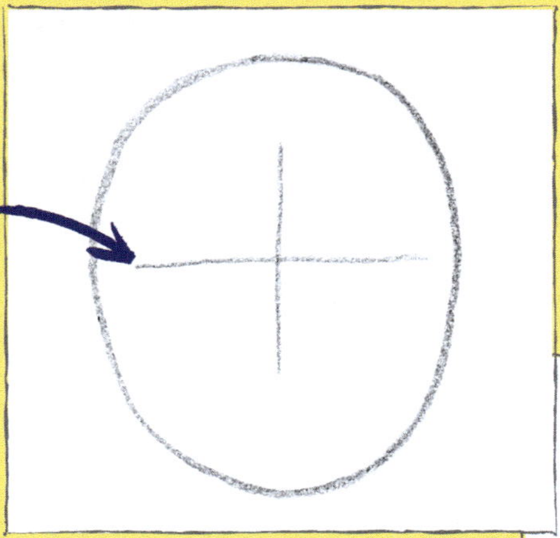

3 Add the hair and ears.

4 Now add bits to the face.

It is a funny face!

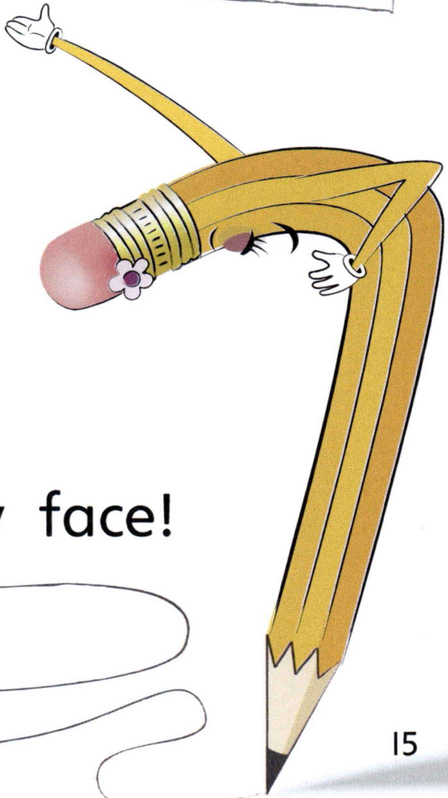

Picture index